X GAMES

Snowboard Superpipe

by Connie Colwell Miller

Content Consultant:
Ben Hobson
Content Coordinator
Extreme Sports Channel
United Kingdom

Reading Consultant:
Barbara J. Fox
Reading Specialist
North Carolina State University

Capstone press
Mankato, Minnesota

Blazers is published by Capstone Press,
151 Good Counsel Drive, P.O. Box 669, Mankato, Minnesota 56002.
www.capstonepress.com

Library of Congress Cataloging-in-Publication Data
Miller, Connie Colwell, 1976–
    Snowboard superpipe / by Connie Colwell Miller.
    p. cm.—(Blazers. X games.)
    Includes bibliographical references and index.
    ISBN-13: 978-1-4296-0110-8 (hardcover)
    ISBN-10: 1-4296-0110-8 (hardcover)
    1. Snowboarding—Juvenile literature. 2. ESPN X Games—Juvenile
literature. I. Title. II. Series.
GV857.S57M54 2008
796.939—dc22   2007001743

Summary: Describes the sport of snowboard superpipe, focusing on the
    X Games competitions and star athletes.

Essential content terms are bold and are defined at the bottom of the page where they first appear.

Editorial Credits
Mandy R. Robbins, editor; Bobbi J. Wyss, designer; Jo Miller, photo researcher

Photo Credits
Corbis/Jeff Curtes, 13; NewSport/Ben Burgeson, 28–29; Reuters/
    Rick Wilking, 12
Getty Images Inc./Doug Pensinger, cover
Red Bull Photofiles/Christian Pondella, 11
SportsChrome Inc/Rob Tringali, 22–23
ZUMA Press/K.C. Alfred/SDU-T, 6; Tony Donaldson/Icon SMI, 5, 9, 27;
    USP/Justin Kase Conder, 14, 15, 17, 19, 20, 21, 25

1 2 3 4 5 6 12 11 10 09 08 07

Table of Contents

A Perfect Run 4

Superpipe Basics 10

Taking the Gold 16

The Best of the Pipe 24

Superpipe Diagram 22

Glossary 30

Read More 31

Internet Sites 31

Index 32

A Perfect Run

In January 2006, excited fans lined a snowy slope in Aspen, Colorado. Snowboarder Shaun White took off down the superpipe.

White caught huge air.
Then he soared into a 900-degree
and a 1080-degree spin. But he
wasn't finished yet. By the end of his
run he'd spun an amazing 14 times!

BLAZER FACT

To spin in one full circle
is 360 degrees. A 1080 is
three full circles.

White slid down the pipe to the finish line. Fans screamed. Cameras clicked. White's flawless run scored him the gold medal at the 2006 Winter X Games.

BLAZER FACT

Shaun White won the gold medal in snowboard superpipe and slopestyle at the 2003 and 2006 Winter X Games.

Superpipe Basics

A superpipe looks like a giant pipe with its top half sliced off. Snow coats both sides of the pipe. The top edges are called lips.

lip

Superpipes have high, straight walls
that launch riders into the air. Riders
cruise down the middle of the pipe to
gain speed. They coast up and out of the
pipe to do tricks.

Derek Heidt

BLAZER FACT

Superpipe walls are at least 16 feet (4.9 meters) tall.

Athletes perform tricks with names like the **McTwist**. They grab the edges of their boards in midair. They change direction and rotate their bodies.

McTwist (mick-TWIST)—a trick done in the air where a rider rotates one and a half times while his or her front hand grabs the toe side of the board

Taking the Gold

Riders don't get many chances to impress the judges. Most **competitions** only have two runs.

competition (kom-puh-TISH-uhn)–a contest between two or more people

Luke Wynen

Judges rate each run on style and difficulty of tricks. They also rate athletes on how much air they catch. The rider with the highest score wins.

BLAZER FACT

There are at least 35 superpipes in the United States.

Kelly Clark

Superpipe athletes win medals and cash prizes for top finishes. Cash prizes can be as much as $15,000.

Torah Bright

Superpipe Diagram

lip

wall

starting line

The Best of the Pipe

Top riders like Shaun White and **Antti Autti** meet up each year. They compete at the Winter X Games and the World Superpipe Championships.

Antti Autti (AN-tee OW-tee)—a snowboarder from Finland

Antti Autti

AMES

Mason Aguirre is another star athlete. At just 18 years old, he won the 2006 World Superpipe Championship. As the sport of superpipe grows, more fans and daredevil athletes are sure to follow.

Mason Aguirre (MASE-on a-GEAR-ee)—a snowboarder from Duluth, Minnesota

Mason Aguirre

Catching Big Air!

Glossary

athlete (ATH-leet)—a person who competes in a sport

championship (CHAM-pee-uhn-ship)—a contest among the best athletes

competition (kom-puh-TISH-uhn)—a contest between two or more people

McTwist (mick-TWIST)—an aerial trick where a rider rotates one and a half times while his or her front hand grabs the toe side of the board

rotate (ROH-tayt)—to spin around

slope (SLOHP)—a slanted surface or hill; people snowboard on slopes.

slopestyle (SLOHP-stile)—a type of snowboarding where the rider chooses his or her own route through a course that has bumps, rails, and jumps

Read More

Firestone, Mary. *Extreme Halfpipe Snowboarding Moves.* Behind the Moves. Mankato, Minn.: Capstone Press, 2004.

Kalman, Bobbie, and Kelley MacAulay. *Extreme Snowboarding.* Extreme Sports No Limits. New York: Crabtree, 2004.

Internet Sites

FactHound offers a safe, fun way to find Internet sites related to this book. All of the sites on FactHound have been researched by our staff.

Here's how:
1. Visit *www.facthound.com*
2. Choose your grade level.
3. Type in this special code **1429601108** for age-appropriate sites. You may also browse subjects by clicking on letters, or by clicking on pictures or words.
4. Click on the **Fetch It** button.

FactHound will fetch the best sites for you!

Index

Aguirre, Mason, 26
Aspen, Colorado, 4
Autti, Antti, 24

competitions, 4–8, 16,
    24, 26

fans, 4, 8, 26

judges, 16, 18

medals, 8, 20

prizes, 20

riders, 4, 12, 15, 16,
    18, 24
runs, 4, 7, 8, 16, 18

scoring, 18
snowboarders. *See*
    riders
speed, 12
superpipe, 4, 8, 10,
    12, 13, 18, 26
    finish line, 8
    lips, 10
    walls, 12, 13

tricks, 7, 12, 15, 18

White, Shaun, 4–8, 24
World Superpipe
    Championships,
    24, 26